Judy Thompson-Phillips

Carolina Gardens & Lighthouses
A Classic Coloring Book for Adults

Carolina Gardens & Lighthouses
A Classic Coloring Book for Adults

©2016 Judy Thompson-Phillips
All rights reserved. No part of this publication
may be reproduced or transmitted in any form
or by any means, electronic or mechanical,
including photocopy, recording or any information
storage and retrieval system, without permission
in writing from the artist.
Contact author/artist; judy@jthompsonart.com

Also by Judy Thompson-Phillips:
Charleston: Classic Coloring Book for Adults
ISBN 9780692586440

to ORDER
http://www.amazon.com/dp/069258644X

Page left blank for no pen bleed through.

Hatteras Lighthouse, NC

Page left blank for no pen bleed through.

Page left blank for no pen bleed through.

Cape Lookout Lighthouse, NC

Page left blank for no pen bleed through.

Page left blank for no pen bleed through.

Ocracoke Island Lighthouse, NC

Page left blank for no pen bleed through.

Wilmington Shrimp Boats

Page left blank for no pen bleed through.

Flame Azalea

Page left blank for no pen bleed through.

Page left blank for no pen bleed through.

Brookgreen Path

Page left blank for no pen bleed through.

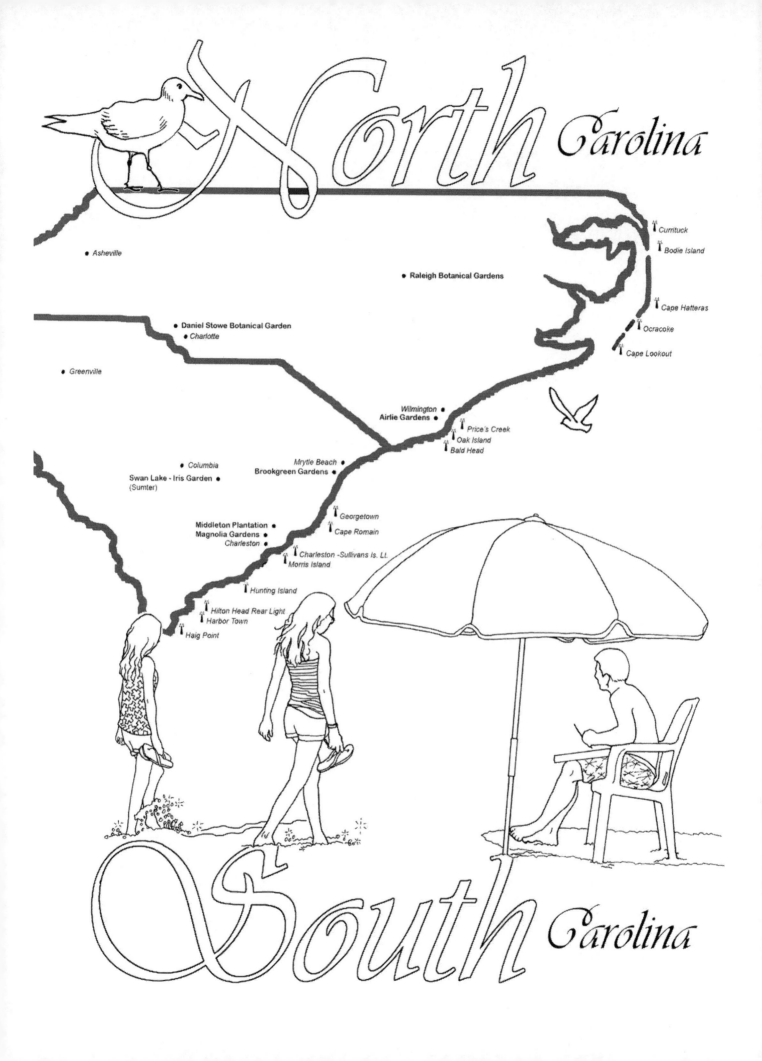

Page left blank for no pen bleed through.

Hunting Island Lighthouse, SC

Page left blank for no pen bleed through.

Middleton Place Vista

Page left blank for no pen bleed through.

Harbour Town Lighthouse, SC

Page left blank for no pen bleed through.

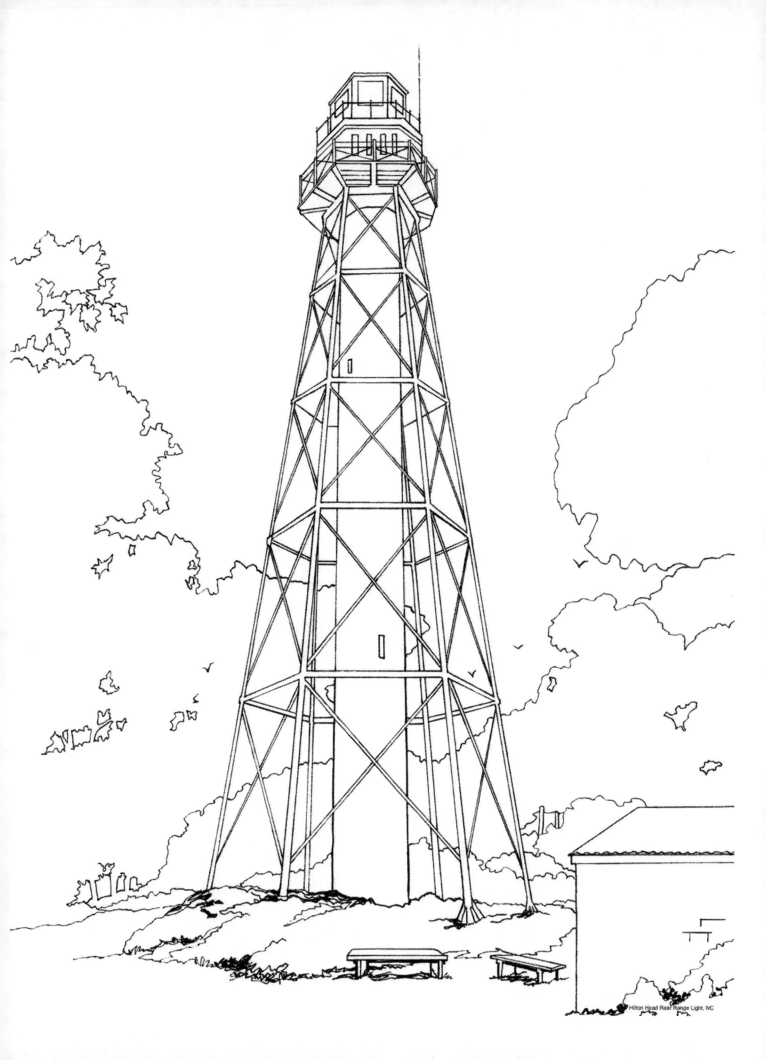
Hilton Head Rear Range Light, NC

Page left blank for no pen bleed through.

Charleston (Sullivan's Island) Lighthouse

Page left blank for no pen bleed through.

Page left blank for no pen bleed through.

Georgetown Lighthouse, SC

Page left blank for no pen bleed through.

Haig Point Lighthouse, SC

Page left blank for no pen bleed through.

Orchid Pool, D.S.B. Gardens

Oak Island Lighthouse, NC

Page left blank for no pen bleed through.

Magnolia Plantation Bridge

Page left blank for no pen bleed through.

Bodie Lighthouse, NC

Page left blank for no pen bleed through.

Currituck Lighthouse, NC

Page left blank for no pen bleed through.

Angel Trumpet, Raleigh Botanical Gardens

Page left blank for no pen bleed through.

Price's Creek Old Lighthouse, NC

Page left blank for no pen bleed through.

Sunflowers, roadside

Page left blank for no pen bleed through.

Morris Island Lighthouse, SC

Page left blank for no pen bleed through.

Color these pages "*YOUR WAY*" or look to hints below.

Bald Head Island
North Carolina's first lighthouse, "Old Baldy", was built in 1795. A majestic octagonal structure, raising ninety feet, it's brick walls are a sturdy five feet thick. Passenger ferry service only to the island.

The walls are a motley blend of beige-tans giving a camuflodge look. Purple flowering butterfly bushes have been planted against a white picket fence.

Bodie Lighthouse
Local folklore says the island got its name from the many **bodies** that washed ashore from shipwrecks. Thirty-five miles north of Cape Hatteras, the beacon served to guide many ships through "the graveyard of the Atlantic", a name given to the treacherous waters.

The lighthouse is in alternating bands of black and white creating a striking look against your version of sky.

Brookgreen Gardens
"Happiness", a 1982 gift by sculptor Nancy DuPont Reynolds; is located in a children's garden, surrounded in a dazzling display of tulips and fauna. The gardens have 9,100 acres that have been developed into a premiere display of sculpture and fragrant flora.

Choose color in varying tones for the tulips. The background greens, a bluer tint, a bit of olive green, in front. The sculpture is in gray.

Brookgreen Path
Beauty is everywhere one looks at Brookgreen, a fantasy land of old plantations, Spanish moss, flower fragrance and world class sculptures intermingle in breathtaking settings. As a child this was my first exposure to art, I guess it made an impression.

The azaleas on the left: shades of pink-red, the gate black with blue or brown in places, orange bits beyond gate and white profusion in shrubbery.

Cape Lookout Lighthouse
Built in 1859. Located on Cape Lookout National Seashore, the lighthouse can only be reached by passenger ferry or can be seen from Harkers Island.

A distinct diamond pattern in black and white is beautiful against a rich colored sky. The grayed areas are shades of black.

Cape Romain Light
Located between Charleston and Georgetown the lighthouse is on seventy-five acre Lighthouse Island and part of a 65,000-acre Wildlife Refuge. The site is not accommodating to visitors and has insects aplenty.

The color is white with vertical stripes of black alternating on the upper two-thirds.

Carolinas Botanical
Just a few well known flowers of the Carolinas. The border may be colored as stained glass or trellis.
Indigo, famous blue, shows in it's blossoms. Carolina Rose has pink tones, yellow center. Honeysuckle is yellow, strong pink at tips. Pokeberries are redddish black. Muscadines, purple blue or green. Jasmine, yellow. Azalea, reds-pinks.

Currituck Lighthouse
The last lighthouse built on the Outer Banks (1875). About a million bricks were needed and, probably to save money, they were never painted. The beacon can be seen up to nineteen miles away.
Color: mute the red brick or it will dominate the page, sky colors need to be deep.

Color these pages *"YOUR WAY"* or look to hints below.

Daniel Stowe Botanical- "Orchid Pool"

Located near Charlotte, NC, this large garden surprises and delights. The orchid conservatory contains so many colorful species of plants; it's wonderful for a winter day escape, gardens can be enjoyed year round.

The deep color of the pool contrasts against the off white of the columns. Orchids are fuchsia, some broad leaves are edged in pink, planter is very blue.

"Diana"

The founder of Brookgreen Gardens, sculptress Anna Hyatt Huntington's beautiful "Diana of the Chase" is placed in a reflecting pool filled with blooming water irises. Many more of her marvelous sculptures will be found in the gardens along with Rodin and Remington.

Shades of gray highlight Diana, dull brick red at the base, water is brownish-green. Irises are purple-blues with greens. Close-up water reflects sky color.

Flame Azalea

Azaleas come in so many varieties it's easy to see why many southern gardens feature them. This azalea is a spindly bush with intense fragrance and has a place in my garden.

(Azaleas can be colored in any red-pink-yellow of your choice.) Each blossom of my plant has yellows at its base and deep pink at the tip, flame-like. Red rhododendrons' upper right. Doodle in-between if you like.

Georgetown Lighthouse

Georgetown, established in 1732, needed a lighthouse to guide the many ships exporting more rice at the time than any other port in the world! The brick structure stands eighty-seven feet tall and the light is on night and day due to no timing mechanism.

The lighthouse is painted white but may be colored with a tint of sky color; let's say a sunset with orange or cool blues when you want a rainy day picture.

Haig Point Lighthouse

The foundation outline of former plantation home was uncovered during reconstruction in 1986. The light is visible from over nine miles away and is solar battery powered. Today the lights are a private aid to navigation and a guest house of International Paper.

The house is white with cast shadows of blue to purple tints. The large tree looks good in autumn foliage with falling leaves at its base.

Harbour Town

Mostly decorative, this functioning lighthouse is a symbol of Harbour Town Marina on Hilton Head Island. Standing ninety feet tall, it was completed in 1970. The tower is open daily and affords a wonderful view of the marina and surrounding area.

The lighthouse observation deck is painted red, alternating stripes of white and red below. Show bits of these colors in the water reflection below the tower.

Cape Hatteras

America's tallest brick lighthouse at 187 feet was moved to its present location in 1999 due to the dangerous, erosion changing waters of Diamond Shoals, a 12 mile sand bar where two ocean rivers meet.
Stripes alternate black and white, with the base being tan block and red brick center on each section of its octagonal base.

Hilton Head-Rear Range

One of only a few skeletal towers still in existence. The rear light was used to line up exactly with the front beacon to guide ships into the channel. It is located at the eighth hole of the Palmetto Dunes Resort golf course.

The small building is of red brick; by using warm colors in the sky it unifies the picture.

Color these pages *"YOUR WAY"* or look to hints below.

Hunting Island Light
The current lighthouse erected in 1875 is made of cast iron plates and designed to be moved in case of erosion, which indeed happened. Today the lighthouse serves as a landmark for those traveling the interesting Intercoastal Waterway.

The top portion is painted black with white on the lower half. Coloring the fence boards as backlit allows shadow colors on it and below the on the grass.

Magnolia Garden-Bridge
A favorite location, the bridge is captured in countless photos. Magnolia has a more natural approach to maintaining its gardens and has been owned by the same family for over three centuries. Many floral favorites are to be enjoyed here.

Magnolia leaves are deep shinny green, the blossom is creamy-white, the center beige with bits of red. The water is dark and reflective of the bridge.

Carolinas
The map is to serve as memory of good times and general guide to the gardens and lighthouses of the Carolinas.

Color or doodle memories, real or imagined. If we can't be where we dream of, we can pretend!

Middleton Place -Vista
May is the ideal time to visit for the profusion of azalea blooms and fragrance just envelops you. There is always something to see or experience there.

Shown in the drawing are three sections of water, darkest is closer. Blooms range from white to vibrant magenta, shadows could be deeper blue greens.

Middleton Place -Tour
This expansive 65 acres is America's oldest landscaped gardens. History seeps into you at every turn. The working plantation stable yards have sheep that roam, ducks, peacocks and exquisite gardens.

The horses were light-medium brown, sheep a pale dusty gray, sparse grass near them, house dull red brick and shadows gray-purple.

Morris Island Light
Time and tide eroded away today, Morris Island is just a lighthouse base now. Close to the eastern end of Folly Beach (my home for many years) is the best view of this restored 161-ft. tall lighthouse. Parking is scarce. Folly's beach is popular, wide and lovely.

Black top, the first stripe of creamy white alternates with brown. Water reflects sky color in deeper tones.

Oak Island Lighthouse
Built in 1958 with 2,500,000 candlepower; it is one of the most powerful and last manually operated lighthouses in the world. The structure's concrete has color mixed into it and never needs repainting. It's near the state's biggest port, Wilmington.

The top is black, then off-white band, base; soft brown band.

Ocracoke Lighthouse
Legend says Blackbeard the pirate met his death at Ocracoke in 1718. His treasure is still being sought today. Made of brick covered with plaster it rises 75 feet tall with five feet thick base.

The white lighthouse reflects into the water as well as the sky colors with a slightly deeper tone.

Color these pages "*YOUR WAY*" or look to hints below.

Price's Creek Light
Built along the Cape Fear River in 1849, the only one of the early river lights that exists today after enduring shell damage during the Civil War. It tells the passing of time and history. I placed a white egret at its base and sailboats to suggest life goes on.

The red of the bricks needs to be in varying shades and roughly done with similar color grasses intermixed with greens.

Raleigh Botanical Gardens
Angel Trumpet has oversize blossoms and can reach fifteen feet tall with a most delightful fragrance. The many botanical gardens are a must see treat when you are near one.

The blossoms range from a peachy-pink to a creamy white, The leaves are various tones of green… or invent your own variety… you're the artist!

Sullivans Island- Charleston Light
The last tower built in the state in 1962; it replaced the old Morris Island lighthouse. The unusual modern triangular shape was built to withstand hurricanes and stands 163-feet tall. There is much to see and do nearby.

The top is black with white at bottom. With strong colored skies, the birds standout in the picture.

Sunflowers
Old barns and wildflowers dot the rural landscape of the Carolinas' and you're sure to see many such sights if you travel on some of the byways between destinations.

Sunflowers are varying shades of yellow-gold, the leaves a medium green. Vary the color in everything you color and, to unify the picture, include bits of neighboring color on nearby objects.

Sumter- Swan Lake & Iris Garden
Seeing black water reflecting white swans is a breath taking sight. Add the profusion of irises, daylilies, cyprus trees in the water and more and the trip is worth it!

The irises are shades of purple-pink-blue, a bit of golden yellow as the petal unfurls; their leaves various shades of green with an occasional orange-brown leaf for color. Swans are cool blue tint to creamy below.

Wilmington-Cape Fear
The shrimp boats were a familiar sight along the coasts but fewer boats make their living here now as pollution and over-fishing take their toll. (Miss Yvette, a real shrimp boat, was named after my daughter.)

Boats are whatever color you want, most have white from the top rail to the line below. The heron is in shades of gray with yellow feet. Water has sky reflections.

A Carolina native, Judy Thompson-Phillips is a life long artist, starting very young with crayons and coloring books and now, *full circle back to coloring books!* There were so many wonderful scenes to choose from in making this book, it was almost an impossible task. You will find your own favorite places when next you tour our beautiful Carolinas.

A fine artist, Judy has original paintings, limited edition Giclee prints, notecards and mugs, most with a Carolina influence.

"I truly hope you enjoy the pages in this book as much as I did making it for you"
Judy

Bonus Page
Sketch / sample colors

Bonus Page
Sketch / sample colors